*Growing
Back*

Publication of this book was supported by a grant from the
Eric Mathieu King Fund of The Academy of American Poets.

THE

James

DICKEY

CONTEMPORARY POETRY SERIES

EDITED BY RICHARD HOWARD

Growing Back

Poems 1972–1992

Rika Lesser

18 March 1998
De Salm

Rika Lesser

UNIVERSITY OF SOUTH CAROLINA PRESS

Other Books by Rika Lesser

Poetry

Etruscan Things   1983
All We Need of Hell   1995

Poetry in Translation

Holding Out (Poems of Rainer Maria Rilke)   1975
Hours in the Garden and Other Poems by Hermann Hesse   1978
Guide to the Underworld by Gunnar Ekelöf   1980
Rilke: Between Roots   1986
A Child Is Not a Knife: Selected Poems of Göran Sonnevi   1993
What Became Words: Poems by Claes Andersson   1996

Retellings for Children

Hansel and Gretel (Illustrated by Paul O. Zelinsky)   1984
My Sister Lotta and Me (Swedish text by Helena Dahlbäck,
pictures by Charlotte Ramel)   1993

Published in Columbia, South Carolina, by the
University of South Carolina Press

Manufactured in the United States of America

01 00 99 98 97   5 4 3 2 1

Library of Congress Cataloging-in-Publication Data

Lesser, Rika.
    Growing back : poems, 1972–1992 / Rika Lesser.
        p.   cm. — (The James Dickey contemporary poetry series)
    ISBN 1–57003–232–7 (cl). — ISBN 1–57003–233–5 (pb)
    I. Title. II. Series.
    PS3562.E837G76 1997
    811'.54—dc21   97–21149

for Paul O. Zelinsky

and

for Göran Sonnevi

Contents

A Note on Rika Lesser

Many of the poems offered here were plausibly intended to constitute the poet's first book, and may well be taken, thus proemially, as lections of the poet's early life (in terms of gestures outward—"away," she calls it—from family, school, comradely intimacy); *initiating* that tussle with narcissism of which the outcome, if not the solution, is either love or death; *developing* her own dramatic rituals of restraint; and *consummating* a pensive and covenantal reverence for the wonders of the self as refracted, most profitably, in landscape or the sea.

But it was not to be so, however plausible, however *intentional*. In 1983, the poems of *Etruscan Things* broke through, as Rika Lesser tells us, and declared themselves "a more satisfactory whole to my sensibility at the time." It proved, of course, a satisfactory whole to other sensibilities too—as James Merrill attested, "these somberly glowing meditations brought a whole world—its gods, artifacts, plunderers—to language and to life." And after a whole world, or at least a satisfactory whole, the poet was on, as we say, to other things, other oppositions to things . . .

Having proved in her preferred archeology how the lineaments of a buried life can be recovered—disinterred and upon such exposure apprehended by the merely living, the merely contemporary—Rika Lesser ventured upon a much more perilous dig, framing a risky archeology of the self which requires not only evidence but testimony, not only comment but restoration. *All We Need of Hell* (1995) afforded glimmerings of identity recovered, got by a loving heart—I myself characterized it on the jacket as "the instauration of enlightened home rule," cautious about calling anything fragmentary that looked so fragmentary as all that. (When we ask what holds poems together, the derisive echo is that poems are held together by what we think holds them together; it is quite an admonishment to education.)

The French have a phrase, *la clef des champs*, "the key to the fields," which key, given or even violently taken, bestows freedom. The present book, restored to its place in the forsaken order of her work, is the key to Rika Lesser's fields as to her enigma ("it is departure always that amazes"). *Growing Back*, as she proleptically calls it, demonstrates—as these things are demonstrated poetically, not biographically—that it takes more than relentless questioning, more than the positing of ironic skepticism as the prolegomenon to any future therapeutics, to get the reader, and the author, from the excavated Etruria of that first book to the intransigent excantation of that second one.

Much evidence, or method, of the transition is in the title poem, surely the triumph of her (early) makings. Having already expressed her devotions to Rilke, to Vermeer, to Ekelöf, northern masters who remain her resource (and her reproach), it is by "growing back" that Rika Lesser gains her saying:

> It grows all too clear, what I set out to do without
> ambition and beyond reward. I have taken too many
> into my keeping, careful to possess none.
> To keep my balance: this distance. I am exhausted
> not fatigued. When I pass a mirror I haven't the strength
> to look. I am still tempted to believe the heart
> does nothing but pump blood, the hand touches nothing
> it does not disturb. I want to walk weary, naked
> in the night, under clear stars, on a path unfolding
> with each step. . . .

These are the ardors, illusions, and disillusions of Imogen and Marina, those diligent Shakespearean daughters who triumph over themselves so singularly as women. It is in this book that we discern the proper lineaments of an identity, eloquent, heartbreaking even, and not to be trifled with.

Richard Howard

Acknowledgments

The poems in this work were previously published—at times in slightly different form—as follows; grateful acknowledgment is made to the editors of the journals and anthologies in which they appeared:

Journal Publication

American Review
　　"The News & The Weather"
　　"Departures"
Caprice
　　"No History"
Earth's Daughters
　　"Under the Roof"
Hubbub
　　"Khalaf-al-Akhmar, the Truth-Liar"
Kalliope
　　"18 December"
Massachusetts Review
　　"Ein Geliebtes: The Body of the Work"
　　"Prescriptions from Sleeplessness"
The Nation
　　"Away"
The New Yorker
　　"527 Cathedral Parkway"
Niagara Magazine
　　"Heartsblood"
Poetry
　　"Translation"
　　"Losses"

Prairie Schooner
   "Growing Back"
   "Vaerøy"
   "Subtexts"
Salamander
   "Interviews"
Shenandoah
   "Joachim and Anna"
   "Of Woman Born"
Western Humanities Review
   "The Amy Lowell Voluntary Exile"

Book or Anthology Publication

"The Gifts" first appeared in *The Poets' Calendar for the Millennium* (Los Angeles: Sun & Moon Press, 1997), edited by Douglas Messerli.

"Translation" was reprinted in *The Poetry Anthology 1912–1977* (Boston: Houghton Mifflin, 1978), edited by Daryl Hine and Joseph Parisi.

"Departures" is from *All We Need of Hell*, published in 1995 by the University of North Texas Press.

"527 Cathedral Parkway" was reprinted in *New York: Poems* (New York: Avon, 1980), edited by Howard Moss.

"The News & The Weather" was reprinted in *The Morrow Anthology of Younger American Poets* (New York: Quill, 1985), edited by David Bottoms and Dave Smith.

"CAN ZONE or THE GOOD FOOD GUIDE" first appeared in *New Directions in Prose & Poetry 48* (New York: New Directions, 1984). It was reprinted in *The Morrow Anthology of Younger American Poets* (New York: Quill, 1985), edited by David Bottoms and Dave Smith.

The lines from A. R. Ammons's *Tape for the Turn of the Year* that appear in the poem "PAGES TOWARD THE TURN OF THE YEAR" are reprinted with the permission of his publisher, W. W. Norton & Co., Inc.

Away

Translation

Lost: the Original, its Reason and its Rhyme,
Words whose meanings do not change through time,
"The soul in paraphrase," the heart in prose,
Strictures or structures, meter, *les mots justes;*
"The owlet umlaut" when the text was German,
Two hours of sleep each night, hapax legomenon,
A sense of self, fidelity, one's honor,
Authorized versions from a living donor.

Found in translation: someone else's voice:
Ringing and lucid, whispered, distant, true,
That in its rising accents falls to you,
Wahlverwandtschaft, a fortunate choice,
A call to answer, momentary grace,
Unbidden, yours; a way to offer praise.

The Amy Lowell Voluntary Exile

to Richard Howard

Framgången 203–41, Göteborg
1 December 1974. My dear boy!

Why is it always so difficult to begin, finding
oneself floundering in apology, inventing
excuses where there has been no offense, as if silence
were not golden; or in formality, only to
affirm familiarity's bonds? There is much to be said
for form. You've said most of it, so I'll apologize
in advance if I seem an echo. But when one listens,
when one has heard, one becomes more than a sounding
        board,
or the forest in which the tree falls, more than a mirror,
more than a marionette—

To begin, there's a felicity I keep forgetting
to inform you of: *Framgången,* the lane on which I dwell,
means "success." In my Germanic confusion (more likely
Romanic lassitude), I took it for *Fortschritt,* but I
have progressed. One night, listening to *Sveriges Radio,*
I heard of *Händels framgång* in "some city," which took me
aback: three steps east to the shelves of lexicons. Every
error being germane, I take this correction as some
sign of accommodation, crossing the threshold of tongues

that are tied. I'm learning to hold mine now—an endeavor
others should take up . . . But I must say, it would be easier
    to live
elsewhere: the nearest street, *Utlandagatan*, speaks
more to my condition. Why, in the last three days, I've
    been
taken for Mexican, Filipino, Italian, Greek—
These Nords simply can't recognize a New York Jew! And
    while
I'm expected to tell one Vasa from the next, with all
the intricacies of inbreeding and imperialism,
if one asks, "Have you been to the States?"—to New York,
    not
Minnesota—it turns out they can't see the buildings for
the skyline. So, when I'm not running from those who find
    me
exotic, I find myself singing the praises of the Met.
"But where did your parents come from?" That's when the
    great
Brooklynian I AM won't be contained one moment more,
and the chant of free-footedness, of transparency
rises. You'd think they would understand, what with
    wanderlust.
What is so frightening about seeing through?

One makes friends nonetheless, even among Social Demo-
    crats,
even among advocates of *språkvård* (the affliction of lost
inflections I call it): The poor souls, desperate to maintain
some vestige of identity by reverting to roots!

It is not of *Heimweh* I suffer, just deprivation:
I've had to stop answering the door. The number of
   Mormons,
magazine-mongers, young Commies collecting for the
   North
Vietnamese, small boys knocking on Sunday mornings with
Göteborgs Posten (best to wrap shrimp shells in), amounts to
an Invasion of Privacy one might file suit against in
our City (sparing the Girl Scouts and the Fuller Brush
   Man).
Is Göteborg a city?

It is a port. There is always the sea. And while I may
not cross the Atlantic for some seven months now, I have
learned to cross the ocean of myself, passable
in every weather. The days are short enough, nights quiet.
I have time to read the *O.E.D.*, the Old Testament,
fuss with Ekelöf (as dear a crank as Rilke), marvel
at how I keep being found by poets whose languages
are not "mother" tongues at all.
                    One complaint—Lucky
Strikes are dreadfully expensive: rolling Niemeyer Samson,
   made
in Norway, shipped through Groningen, "a blend of . . .
   ripe golden
Virginia and rich brown Kentucky." Regards to Broadway.
To you, love, ever, *Rika.*

Prescriptions from Sleeplessness

for Gina Riddle

It being 5 A.M., damp,
"regn och blåst," dark now as it will be much
less than twelve hours hence, too cold to swim
"over" the canal, this twenty-second
                day of December,
                vintersolståndet,
I am, as usual, up,
under friendlier waters, in the bath,
hoping to work up a drowsiness, but
neither drop off, nor upset the well of
                delible ink, pre-
                dictably balanced
on the tub's rim. Because you
have chosen to live with another, I
dare not phone, not now. But now that it *is*
so dark here so much of the time, I find
                myself sleepless and
                immersed in those poems
of Ekelöf which begin:
"Ensam i tysta Natten," not because
Night seems Feminine and Divine, not for
quirks of grammar or of men. Night is not
                my sister, nor is
                it my brother, just

another space in which I
go on (or "up"). Besides, if I phoned you,
you would reproach my sleeplessness with those
dreams of yours. Dreams are not to be spoken
                              even to one's most
                              intimate friend. They
are all we possess, while they
possess us, to be read by the silent
reader, alone in the quiet night. Let
                      them go. Give them up.
                      Return them to their
respective archives. Even the
most beautiful, the terrifying
ones. I've been told that I talk in my sleep,
more often unintelligibly than
                              eloquently. I've
                              thought of hiring a
bedfellow who takes shorthand
and has a keen ear. But the scratching of
pencils or the sound of breathing would buy
nothing but my silence. It is all
                      I can do to catch
                      forty winks alone.
Physicians say I suffer
from insomnia (induced perhaps by
anemia). I say habit and add
chacun à . . . , or, better, each one to her
                      sheets! I'm keeping lists—
                      words and expressions—

mistakes Swedes make in English.
Unintentional errors are never
original, just rules not properly
remembered: "He don't," "she are," progressive
                    loss of distinction,
                    of number, not too
odd in a country where the etymological dictionary
(the Academy's!) ends two-thirds through "S."
A loss more grim than Finland. Better still
                    is "isolated":
                    Against cold my flat
may well not be, but I am.
You've heard these things before, more often than
I have; you've spent three winters here. But one
must learn to hear (though this may not be taught)
                    not what one wants to
                    but what strikes the ear,
what is unavoidably
audible, stripped of disguises, seldom
caresses, is quite clear. Forget all this
hogwash. Set the *julskinka* aside. Rise
                    early. Catch number
                    4 toward Mölndal.
When the tram's done weaving—you
won't notice if you don't look outside—do
come directly, like a somnambulist,
I'll have washed the sleep from my eyes at least
                    until sunrise. Please
                    remember the yeast.

If you will train my wrists to
the warmth of formulas, I will knead. We
can drink cappuccino, break open a
carton of Kex, drill our declensions—I'll
                do the kneading, teach
                you how to decline need.

Losses

for Gunnar Ekelöf (1907–1968)

1. A Photograph

Before you on the table, a room you wanted
to describe. One of those bronzed decors with cut-glass
chandelier, low paneling, a restless Turkish rug.
It is *vårvinter*, spring in the power of winter.
Furniture: gilded, late-Gustavian,
embroidered, pinstriped, stuffed. A wooden tabletop
rests on bent-legged 8's cut off at the bottom and top.
Past the portraits and sagas turned copperplates,
past the one of Odysseus—the piano clenches
its teeth at the windows. The light hesitates.
Even the photograph turns its back on the windows.

Inside, your father, one more silent witness,
plunged in a rococo fauteuil,
perched on a pile of comforters,
in morning jacket, stiff. Someone has wedged
a white napkin between his collar and chin.
The forehead high, the eyebrows prominent,
the nose short and straight, the chin strong.
The eyes look out at the photographer,
who is not there, as if to follow
what he does or did, but they are lost

11

in thought, subhuman, fragmentary. Inside
his cool forehead, a swarming coral reef.
Thoughts not inhuman, only "horrible."
Horror is meaninglessness.

2. Near the Church of John

In a cold land you were born
and your family moved, during the first
world war, from hotel to hotel, settled
awhile in Stockholm, by the Church of John.
You went home to that room and found him
surrounded by nurses, cheerfully
calling you, "Grandpa, little Grandpa!"
At sundown you stood while the brick red church
threw its red reflection even into
the darkest corner. And the church bells rang.
And you stood there questioning.

Having stained the costly light red Milanese
brocade on one of the chairs a litmus blue,
Having been allowed "to sit with the others
at the table," though the yolk spilled over his chin,
Having brooded, without words, in rising tones
incomprehensible strings . . .
Having used you as an oracle for his psalter,
Having been troubled, humored, lucid, insane, unloved—
Gerhard Ekelöf died of syphilis.

3. Imago

No more than we can forget the fathers
who were not there
can we forgive the mothers who were
but gave no warmth.
On the bed with bronze paws
the same dream returns and returns.
Sleepless we wrap those shreds of blankets
from a city of ruins around us.

Panayía, Holy Virgin, Virgin of Night,
how were we born?
To want, some are born to want.
Átokos, Mother of All, of No One,
what will we come to?
Your mother and your father
Yours only by chance.
Fatumeh, weaning your child,
what must we do?
He who does not hope knows no despair:
Dream the mother you never had.
He who does not doubt believes nothing:
Know the father you never had.
Believe nothing. You will find your name.

Værøy

"The island in the distance . . . is called by the
Norwegians Vurrgh. The one midway is Moskoe. . . .
These are the true names of the places—but why it
has been thought necessary to name them at all is
more than either you or I can understand. . . ."
—E. A. Poe, "A Descent into the Maelström"

The last outpost is on its eastern coast, facing Mosken.
The cries of ravens veer off the telephone poles
which trail off to Mostad, an abandoned fishing village.
A narrow footpath chases the mountain ridges.
Winding along it, you will catch and lose sight of Mosken:
an enormous supine parrot, the sun caught in its beak.
The path is six inches wide and covered with sheep drop-
    pings.
On the left, a wall of mossy crags; on the right, a steep
    drop.
(Sometimes the sheep stumble on the rocks and slide:
tiny white avalanches to the sea.)
The trail winds down to water. The beach is underwater.
You walk on sea-smoothed rocks, watching for dry ones.
Among them, pools of decomposing seaweed,
rust orange pools of rotting sea palms.
Green sponges fringe the undersides of boulders.
A six-toed puffin hound digs for off-white eggs.
At last a marker: Kalkluovnen, the bird-rocks
sculptured and gray, the quicklime furnace.

Within the folds and gorges of Kalkluovnen
the black-backed gulls and razorbill auks all stand
with their beaks toward Greenland
in rows of silhouettes, no two the same.
Rainbow-billed puffins (Norwegians call them "sea-
    parrots")
like flying sausages dive for stippled sea urchins,
while the querulous kittiwakes bicker and screech
shooting off clusters and tufts of feathers.
The North Atlantic eats at a cliff
which becomes a male profile, thirty meters high.
He is "Tussen," a huge troll, and stares over the ocean.
Far above, white-tailed sea eagles float and pass out of
    sight.

Back at the marker, a road opens to Mostad.
Remnants of iron railings guide you; the ground is solid.
The island narrows, you cross back to its east coast.
The interior, westward, is bird-punctured stone.
Across the bay is a white strip of beach called Sanden,
rising from it, a black tabula rasa, one thousand feet high.

Poe saw nothing of this, "giddy, atop Helseggen,"
the knife-edged peak of the goddess whose face is half
    human
half blank. In the province of Nordland, sunlit all summer,
sixty-eight degrees north, beyond the Maelström is Værøy:
Nesting Place, Island of Rams, Weather and Wind.
All this it gives you. Værøy, not Vurrgh, is the given name.

Growing Back

for Judith Hoberman

The overgrown plant, billed as a cactus, but surely
a sedum of sorts: parts of it properly upright,
others, stems, half dead, with persistent tips, clusters
of fleshy leaves trailing the withered pink blooms, effortless,
sessile, removed to a table, since spring will not come
though it's April 14th, the window-ledge battered
by corn-snow, the jambs dropping melted sleet. The plant I
   bought
only one of this year, knowing it would be just
one year I might keep it. It could do with a larger pot
and doubtless will when I give it away. It will be
time to give up every thing again; but now I cling
to these surroundings, can scarcely raise myself from bed
regardless of sleep or time.

In a dream I lent out my lexicons, even
the *O.E.D.* and *Webster's Third New International*,
abandoning these for a diction. Some other voice
than Reason's dictated this. Some other dictator
indited, commanding me leave my stays and enter
a world of forms, spaces, chambers enclosed but roofless,
sands over my head, the sea distant but present.
I never speak in my dreams though I talk in my sleep.
I have never woken screaming. Stifling I've tried
to scream and woken; no incubus perched on my sternum.

Voices I have heard: a word or two spoken sagely,
distinctly, irrevocably; or sounds, birds or bells.
I myself have never answered.

In a dream I removed a particolored blouse
and with it all the color of my bruised arms.
Another: I walked out among rocks, sands and seabrush;
each one spun on its own axis. Wrapped in a caftan,
I tried to reach firm ground, touched something
and covered my face with my hands. When I took them off
they were caked with blood and my face completely
    charred.
This too came off, a black thickness with the mouthprint
still clinging. In another room, girls screamed, women
drew blood from a man's chest, the police were coming . . .
I could not leave that house.

I have been walking in my sleep again. Where I've been
no one knows, but my footsoles smart as if parched
by hot sands. I woke to raining slush, chilled through,
though my feet were burning. I woke and rose only
because something rang, and the ringing disrupted
my hand furiously writing away on the sheet.
What I wrote no one knows. It was a letter
with letters sloping uphill.

Has it been long since I wrote? I can't keep track, had
    counted
on you as clock and calendar. You kept track for me.
I have been down in the caked sand at the shore between
    tides.

Not as the rootless sea palm with its crown of blades,
but as the lug, *Arenicola*, casting a mound of my form
behind, above me. Found nothing. Turned back. —
Out of context, many things can be bridged, nothing
    changed.
And the bridges we think we have burned behind
are more secure than any destination.

Write me again of your wedding, the glow that lit
everyone that day; or of married life, tender
distractions, backgrounds submerged. I want to invent
a new dance, a new ritual, with my own tempo,
somewhat out of time. There will be no music,
just the sequence of words: I begin I begin I begin.
And the dance is a ring, but no hands are joined,
just extended, palms half up, fingers curled inward,
one hand before the other . . .

It grows all too clear, what I set out to do without
ambition and beyond reward. I have taken too many
into my keeping, careful to possess none.
To keep my balance: this distance. I am exhausted
not fatigued. When I pass a mirror I haven't the strength
to look. I am still tempted to believe the heart
does nothing but pump blood, the hand touches nothing
it does not disturb. I want to walk weary, naked
in the night, under clear stars, on a path unfolding
with each step. Nothing more than the mind of the sedum
breathing through its limbs, of the tumbleweed, before
    autumn.

Away

It is departure always that amazes
not the claims of this or some other shore;
many make their homes in distant places.

Changes of light, time, heart, mere commonplaces
against the final closing of a door.
It is departure always that amazes.

Exile is sweet, when chosen, it effaces
all we have learned, reveals what we must explore:
how we can make our homes. In distant places

meanders broaden. All praise is
due those turns we failed to take before.
Bless the departure, always. A maze is

what we make of our lives: impromptu braces
and timbers comfort the Minotaur
who finds himself at sea in open places.

Strange offspring! Our masks, our faces
fall as we strip them bare. What more
than departure possibly could amaze us
who have to make our homes in distant places?

The Gifts

Lyric

Who is this old man
walking through my head?
His room is empty,
My heart his bed.
The bed is mountainous;
He cannot lie down.
Within these mountains
The man is stone.

Departures

In memory of Moris Fogelhut (1888?–1970)

1. *Ich habe Tote, . . .*

The broken chair of wood, of mahogany—the one that used
to be his, with cushions of fluffy gold brocade, changed
by his daughter, later, for something flatter, more
American in pattern, almost colonial, even as he lived
with us in the house; the small oak table with liberty
bells cut out of its sides, two shelves for books or whatnots;
the paired twin beds with bells in bas-relief on the head-
    boards,
missing, burned long ago in another room;
the four-poster he died in, naturally, now mine:
these furnishings rebuke my heedlessness: as if I sinned
the day he died—not practicing piano in the morning
before I left. Reproach me—for not having wept enough,
for not learning the siddur, the mahzor, the Torah—
for keeping appointments, customs, never faith.

Because we name our children for the dead, I am "Rika,"
after his only wife. In our albums she is sturdy and
large-breasted, almost stern. The name, as given to me,
had no meaning. Passed down like a poem conned to rote.
And yet we learn it does mean "limb" in Bulgarian,
"pear blossom" in Japanese, "rich" in Swedish; often

misspelled, and either mispronounced at birth or ever
   since . . .
What is mine by custom is empty of meaning.
Only a word that I must renew. What was I born to:
Galicia, his *glil-ha-goyim*, turned in for a new land,
when and why forgotten. Short-sighted, my grandfather
might fail to recognize me in the street. But how he'd keep
the Sabbath, how his hands would hold the keys to the
   temple.
How he would touch the doorposts when he entered or left.

2. . . . *und ich liess* . . .

Why do you live in Sweden?
>   *Because my work is portable.*
Why?
>   *Because I had a lot to leave.*
What do you speak?
>   *Swedish, English, sometimes German.*
What?
>   *I have not said one word in three months.*
Do you feel safe?
>   *Ja visst!*
Do you?
>   *Only in the dark.*
How do you spend your evenings?
>   *Writing, writing many letters, many words.*
How?
>   *I sleep with a strange man every night.*

In your letters you wrote you had many friends.
In my letters I am given to lies.
In your letters . . .
Yes I had friends; all are dead to me.
Would you prefer that we did not come to see you?
Stay where you are lest you see me as I am.
Would you prefer . . .
Of course you must come, you are all I have left.

3. . . . *sie hin*

Leaving, yes. When I returned that day, he was still warm
with death. He had just asked once more for the plain box
    of pine.
Never having known me as now I am: thinner, full
of languages he had no use for.
He is the old man walking through my head,
a memory scratching like a cane on slate.
Whose was that slogan, *Death will set me free?* Renew,
rejuvenate—words that must expire. If I render them
I do not give them up. These are my words, my landscape,
the peoples I am heir to. All that we have
is not all we possess. We can give twice as much—
like the mirror that upsets us in the morning
consoling us at night. What was it Rilke wrote?

> *We have, where we love, only this:*
> *to release each other, for to hold one another*
> *comes easily to us, and need not be learned.*

To release each other, to widen the freedom
in our poverty we name "love," by giving back,
by returning to what has been freely given.

536 Saratoga Avenue

Driving by it now—walking in Brownsville
is no longer safe—536 remains
the only semi-private house on the block.
Everything else has changed: The tenements
across the street are gone. Nothing
replaces them. On our side, burnt and
blown-out frames surround empty courtyards.

Long before I was born, my mother's family
bought the house. Grandmother Ruchtcha died.
I bear the English name she took at
Immigration. Had she not died, I would be
someone else—a name is powerful.

Sharing a bedroom with my middle sister,
I wondered why the playroom was not my own.
Too young to remember Grandfather's moving
out. He lived nearby, across a busy street,
then in the downstairs flat, then in a "home."
Finally, he lived with us; the playroom his again.

My eldest sister had the long front room.
In the street you knew when she talked
on the telephone: she'd stick her feet
out the jalousie windows. Now a wide
strip of tape masks a bifurcation.

Of course, there were other rooms, other doors,
but one of those farthest back completes the tour.

The full bath was called "Rika's bathroom"
because I hogged it. In my sleep I'd walk there.
Awake I'd drown my toys, imagining the room
to be an island. Shipwrecked, I allowed myself
a large box of cream-filled cookies. With water,
soft towels, the clothing in the hamper,
I'd do all right. I won't allow myself to imagine
what goes on there now. What the small black boy,
who rode a tricycle when we drove past
last summer, would think if he found
scratched with the head of safety-pin
on the tile wall beneath the towel rod
my name.

The Gifts

I

The first box is as long as your arms
and round, a hatbox to take to heart
not head. Inside: a drum, tympanum
that beats by itself for you. When you
run, it works your lungs, and sounds as if
small, well-formed feet danced on its rim.
Place it under your bed; it helps you sleep.
Not manufactured. Comes in one size.
Involuntary and invaluable.

II

If you can unbind all the bands—
for it seems this is a ball of
nothing but them—you may then un-
ravel this sphere of wigs: some long
and loose, some braided and done up,
toward the center, short and shingled.
A disguise for each discomfort.
The core, irrevocably, is
a mirror with no frame or stand,
just a hook at the top. For women only.

III

A single railroad car, on weekends
computerized to run between
Tashkent and Raivola. On weekdays
the decor ranges from watered-silk
chaise longues to velvet davenports.
Entrance: Grand Central, go down several
flights to Lexicon Parvenu Line.
Poets half-rate on round trips at all times.

IV

A set of dictionaries: Swedish-Danish
                               Danish-Portuguese
                               Portuguese-Persian
                               Persian-Armenian
                               Armenian-Sanskrit
                               Sanskrit-Chinese
                               Chinese-English.
All volumes but the first are in preparation
and will be sent by sea, one every three years.

Under the Roof

I am not sleeping and again the sun
is rising. Even the Wandering Jew
raises its arms, as if singing.
"Attack the enemy!" *The Outer Limits*
blares from the screen. An attack
of nerves, or is it habituation?
Sleeplessness—Sweden in winter—
when nights were clearer than days.

Last winter I moved into a building
in Brooklyn Heights, beside
the Lutheran's lone bell, opposite
the Presbyterian's off-key carillon.
The space was calm.
The building had stood a long time.
Across the street the brownstones
are painted numerous shades of red.

I came with a piano and the best
intentions. I came for the high
ceilings, the loft bed, the gas stove,
for the alcove, the recessed windows,
the archways, but hear footsteps
on the ceiling, voices in the bath,
eternities from one day to the next.

An alarm goes off. A voice asks:
—Do you know eternity?
—Do you know eternity?
—Do you know what time it is?
Below my windows they are speaking loud
and their accents are surprising on a Sunday
here in Brooklyn. At the tops of their lungs
German is what they are speaking, waking all
would-be late-sleepers within stone's throw
of the Deutsche-Evangelisch-Luther-Zions Kirche.
Half the church says '39, the other '87,
and the signboard (*Herzlich willkommen*)
reads: Founded in 1855. The bell tolls.
—It must be eleven A.M.

The building has stood a long time.
Through the floors I feel the Hotel
Saint George battle the 7th Avenue Dragon.

527 Cathedral Parkway

Squatting under the weight
of the balcony they support,
four gargoyles in need of cleaning:

The first, hunched over a bowl,
raises a spoon to his gaping mouth—
the Black Hole of Cathedral Parkway.
His right foot has four toes
with lots of dirt between them.
His nose is long, blunt at the tip.
He must be very hungry—lids
lowered, eyes only for his food.

The second is bald, bends
over a book, his filthy beard
caught among the pages. One
eyebrow raised, both eyes dart
to the left; they have a knowing look.
In his right hand a heavy plume.
If he's an artist, the arts are black.

The third, alchemist or cook,
clutches a cauldron. Flames lick
its bottom. He looks younger
than the others, lacks a tooth,
sticks out his tongue, touches
it with a finger.

The fourth, greedy, *very* greedy,
has a whole roast chicken on a platter.
He is not intent on eating, only
on keeping it for himself. His legs
bend in the lotus position; in every
other way he's a dog.

Eastward, their four twin brothers hold up
another balcony, but in a different order:
The Cook, Jack Sprat, Rover, The Leery Sage.
Higher up, over us all,
ten heads as well as two gryphons
drop their blessings on all who pass.

Heartsblood

I

The apricots were sweet—
sweeter, moister than any
in life. Burning, they fell
from my hands, the dried fruit
that were a shade of yellow—
almost orange—more concentrated
than sunrise.

II

There's a taste in my mouth
that is bitter.
You put it there
with your tongue. Afternoons, I
am weak, sleep, wake.
The taste abides like the lace
cloth of snow draped
over rooftops of brownstones.

III

One facade's been denuded:
The ivy vines are stripped, veins
too secret, too vital
to weather exposure.

Across a clean face the shadow
of an unseen bird flying upward
drops down the sunbright stone.

IV

To the poison of your tongue
there is no antidote,
not the dogtooth violet
nodding on its stem:
Erythronium denscanis;
not my own blood liberally
spent. Night after night
I hope to build
a tolerance, grow immune
like Mithradates.

V

In the center of the courtyard
of an insula built over
Nero's rubble, a Mithraic
temple was buried two levels
below the Christian basilica
of San Clemente. On the ancient
altar, carved in bas-relief, Mithras—
a god born of a rock—slays a bull.
The sevenfold initiates
celebrated in a grotto,
whose vault was stuccoed with stars.

From the mouth of the wound the beast's
blood spills, and they say from it sprang
all plants, all animals, all good.

VI

Heartsblood grows close to the ground,
sends runners, needs indirect light,
rich soil, moisture. The flower is
too frail to press; like the anemone
it has no petals, but the sepals are
colored: red, violet, or blue. The plant
grows wild. Its fruits—verdigris
on ruby stems—never ripen, are poison.

Khalaf-al-Akhmar, the Truth-Liar

The first time I saw him it was clear
he was my father even before I knew
him by his thinning hair, by how he spoke
truths I could never grasp but only sense,
unlike my own, his eyes, dissembling, blue,
his forehead marked by lines forming a cross.

I didn't want a father: I was cross.
I didn't notice that the night was clear,
that constellations gathered in the blue-
black emptiness of everything he knew.
But in the darkness I could almost sense
the lie in every twisted word he spoke:

"There is a legend of a man who spoke
lies half his life. One day at the village cross-
roads he wept for truth. This made no sense
to his townsmen. To them it was quite clear
he was lying. Whatever it was he knew,
was being kept from them. Then the blue

waters of his falling tears became blue
torrents that submerged the town. He spoke
of Memory, how on that day he knew
it had left him. —What bridge does one cross
to reach the gate on which ALL CLEAR
is engraved, where every life makes sense?"

After I heard that tale I lost all sense
of time. Years seemed to pass. His dark blue
shadow covered my own. His eyes grew clear,
his forehead smooth; he never spoke
again but pointed to where all roots would cross
then dissolve. That was the land he knew

as his home and prison. It was then I knew
he was Khalaf-al-Akhmar, and a sense
of loss overwhelmed me. I watched him cross,
from the shore of Memory, over a deep blue
flood to a land where no one spoke
aloud because their thoughts were clear.

I knew I had lost a father for the blue
lips of Lethe spoke what I could sense:
Clearly, in death, your paths will cross.

About Men

Ein Geliebtes: The Body of the Work

for Rainer Maria Rilke

1. Approach

Because you were not mine, I approached
you as I would any human being: hesitantly,
close-mouthed, from a distance. You seemed
both alive and dead, and I tried to work you
out from what others said about you.
Others who thought they knew you.
If I think back to our first meeting, our first
encounter, what impressed me most was your way
of walking: precise in every step.
There are, after all, walls between us.
And a background: but I too can see, "a round shard
with a red ground, upon which the taut legs
of a quadriga appear, like the black inscription
over an entrance."

So I returned your call, though at first
you were belligerent, even openly hostile to me:
Taunting me with puns, inventing words, or worse—
altering the old ones, with no respect for grammar.
Not trusting hearsay, I came to you myself
and held on tight until your Protean forms:
dead body of Christ, horses, butterflies,

43

eyelids of black-eyed roses, clear lachrymatories,
fruits, mirrors, angels, gods and God knows what
turned and returned to one thing with no name,
something nameless and unspeakable. Like a magician
of the invisible, a clock without hands, you pointed to
things in you, in me, somewhere between: Images.
My curse on the words!

2. Depths

Like Christ's soul in Hell I plunged wilder
depths, heard cries howl toward me.
When the landscapes vanish, is it
my voice that speaks? Late at night,
in one ruinous flash, like an exhibitionist
you'll say, "I am your sleeper," and disappear.
Then like a painter faced with blanks, knowing
only no color is absolute, I reconstruct
from tone. Kinder than most, you utter
no loud demands, never look hurt, revenge
is not in your nature. But you just stand there,
clear as the Design in a cloudless sky at night,
and just as constant.

You've made your own defense, down to each
dash that punctuates a pause—, where
I hear music, see a rush of rain, feel a power
descending. But not to me; perhaps to me alone.
You delivered me from my chores to my work,
my real address. Some have too little faith.

We approximate in choosing. But are we lost?
We can only lose ourselves. And one good man
encouraged me to sustain our difficult rapport,
one flamboyant man
with the courage of all the French nation.

3. Vows

There are times I think our affair will never work out.
Bonds delude. Ceremonial diction rings false in
my voice. Praise cannot. Fruits rot, fall away:
but sometimes decay brings forth. The tree rises,
green ascends. How often have I had to turn to Root.
So dark down here, if I look up for an instant,
I'm sure to lose you. I must look down
far down within myself, until I become
transparent, and your print, your imprint emerges.
No one can part us. Few can give advice.
You are my crutch as long as I make you walk.
If there's a god in me, may it be the one of song.
May our words be flung into the invisible and there
live. If I turn wayward or willful,
give me your elegies.

Joachim and Anna

after Giotto
the Scrovegni (Arena) Chapel frescoes, Padua

I. The Expulsion from the Temple

A childless man
lying under the curse of the Law
shall not offer sacrifice
to the Lord of the Law.

> Pushed to the edge of the platform
> an old man holds a lamb without blemish
> like an infant in his arms.
> Sarah is far from his thoughts.

A childless man
adding not to the people of God
shall not stand among men
who have begotten sons.

> Within the fold
> a boy takes the priest's blessing.
> Some leave the Temple.
> Some may not enter it.

II. Joachim Retires to the Sheepfold

Disconsolate, the rich-robed Joachim
looks down at nothing, does not see the hound
in his path, white as the cliffs behind him.
Not tall enough to admit a man, the sheepcote
empties, dark as Anna's womb. Two shepherds
pause, exchange a wary look. Kneading his robes,
Joachim's hands are invisible, the palms
let go of prayer. Nature knows
what Joachim does not: The trees
bend toward him, their crowns heavy
with succulence, and full.

III. The Annunciation to Anna

"If he returns, am I to say to him,
as women, barren as I, have said before me:
'Take thou my handmaid
Go in unto her and she shall bear
upon my knees, that I may have children
by her'? I could not rear another
woman's child. The stars beyond this roof—
the seed of Israel—not one is mine."

Robed in gold, Anna kneels among
the effects of marriage: the trousseau chest,
utensils on the wall, the curtain drawn
halfway around the bed. We see her there
like a doll inside a dollhouse. On the porch,

her legs spread wide, the handmaid
plies her distaff, about to drop the spun
thread on the floor. Anna's lips move.
The servant strains to hear.

Filling the bedroom window an angel
interrupts: a downward glance, a finger
raised in reproach: *And was not Sarah*
first mother of your race
barren until her ninetieth year?
When He closes a womb
He may later open it
and show to all that
what is born thereof
is not the fruit of lust
but of divine munificence
For God indeed punishes
not nature, but sin. You,
Anna, shall bear a daughter
and call her name Mary. Go
to Jerusalem, find Joachim
at the Gate of Gold.

IV. Joachim's Sacrifice

A shepherd said:
—What do I see falling from the sky?
A hand, I think. What miracle is this?
And my two hands, as if magnetized,
raised upward against my will.

On hands and knees Joachim scales the hill:
—Whose form is this?—a slender pair of wings
hidden behind shoulders. A woman? It
does not look like Anna. In her hand
a scepter—has she been sent by God?
Her eyes gaze toward me but will not meet mine.
I long for the touch of her right hand
on my brow. I would be blessed.

The altar flares, the fires rise and scorch
the bones of Joachim's sacrifice. Soot-black
an angel speaks: *Though thou detain me*
I will not eat thy bread
If thou wilt make a korban
Offer it unto the Lord
Behold in the flame of the altar
—even now the flame reaching to heaven—
In this flame I ascend.

V. Joachim's Vision

Asleep now, no longer trusting
what he has seen or what shepherds say,
Joachim has a dream:
                 I am alone,
on high ground before the sheepcote.
A dog keeps watch. The sheep are silent,
grazing. Behind me a mountain top
catches gusts of wind. Out of the sky
an angel hastens toward me. I should feel
terror, but its words heal my wound:
      Your wife will conceive
      Your daughter, Mary, of the tribe
      of David, shall bear a son.

The shepherds passed. The dog watched over him.
Joachim woke and made for Jerusalem.

VI. The Meeting

The angels gone, only the memory of them
widens the eyes of the blessed Joachim
and the blessed Anna. She in her golden gown,
he barefoot, draped in blue and pink. With her left
hand she cups his jaw. With his right he clasps
her shoulder. Their figures fuse, like metals,
in a bell.

A crenelated wall, an archway shield them
from onlookers delighted by their kiss.
Nearest the pair, a woman draws a cloak
around her, turns away (when they break free
they will rejoice and worship and go home)
knowing, as we do, that a wall may crack,
a covenant be broken.

Of Woman Born

after Vermeer

Out of two small rooms in Mechelen,
the house in Delft, women poured.
One woman, not one model:
reading a letter, pouring milk,
weighing gold, holding a shiny pitcher
that reflects the selfsame Turkish rug,
blue silk, the chairs studded with brass
and capped with lions' heads.
We trespass her threshold,
a window pouring light that spills
golden over the brass and bread,
gray-white on her headdress, on the pearls
or paper over which she pores.

Kept from the foreground by the furnishings
she stands back in silence
gazing down at the task at hand.
Behind her is a world or parts of one:
a map of Holland, a doorway, a heavy drape,
landscapes or cupids, a wall with nails and holes.
In her face she holds affection back from us
giving it to a mirror or a pane of glass
until she is lost in reflections.
Never beautiful but always full,

she is one with the deeds of light.
She is composed.

Stilleven, motionless model,
nothing about her is hard.
Painted into a corner, secure,
a man's or a maid's intrusion
is no more to her than light.
She may look up from her lute
or out past everything—
surprised but undisturbed.
The gold, the pearls, the mirror
and the scales, her cloak trimmed ermine
her extended arms . . . Within the issuing light
she cannot close the casement
or upset the balance.
The Last Judgment is behind her.
She is coming into life.

The News & The Weather

I rush to the newspapers. Seeking
something current. Weeklies, quarterlies
put timeliness in archives, always
smother me with their musts. I require:
the press in motion, the past kept back,
letterpress, linotype, cuts, relief.
On television, I only grasp
the weather: the fronts and whorls, offshore
Agnes, stagnant, menacing the land.

How to love you here, in this *city*—
Garment workers strip me with their eyes.
We live too much inside: In your flat
only the two front rooms have windows.
The sides of the building are blank brick.
The fire escape sags; its iron base
and ladder end eight feet off the ground.
There is no where to walk. Every
crosslight is yellow—hesitation.

At night the sidewalk mica flashes.
Buses make every other stop. Trains
avoid bridges. The Watchtower waits
for someone to heed its words. Your kiss
inspects each plane of my flesh like an
elevator, emptied, jarring at
every flaw. You give me no words to heed.

I rush to the newspaper. On page
twenty-seven, column three, I read:

"On Lake Titicaca's floor, thousands
of giant frogs have grown for years.
The team of French savants who've found them
swear by their savoriness, and though they
fear the hides won't tan, Bolivians
should can the Leviathans." I run
downstairs. Whirlwinds of children pogo
up the street. Disengaged stairways wake
me to the sky. And I fly,
                              I fly.

PAGES TOWARD THE TURN
OF THE YEAR

Men are

       largely absent from this book
though not entirely, there's
    my father
    my mother's father
        (my father's father left the household when my dad
        and uncle were young; we children saw him rarely,
        called him Big Grandpa; died 1970, hit by a car
        whose driver left the scene)
    the ones who dare not call unless drunk
    my mom's psychiatrist
    Matthew, of course (not straight)
    the wretch who inspired me last spring to write a poem
       called "Shrinking" (now part of this text)
    the one I fell in and out of love with, unable to care for
       anyone but himself

But aren't they *all* like that (indulge me, right now I can't
    afford to qualify) lacking some quality of caring or of
    love, the ability, desire, imagination to change places
    with anyone?
       (Who would, still, in this world, with a woman?)

Or is something wrong with me?
    Intelligent, even beautiful many now say
       (I trust when I hear this from my women friends)
    honest (not always a plus), faithful, brave . . .

Why am I not "involved" with any one?

Something to do with major past gutting flames?

A-B C: Swedish, 15 years older than I, the jealous
        type—I never got my own keys to his
        Gothenburg flat
D E F: Vietnam vet, great in bed, wanted to marry me,
        but not bright enough, and apt to go off, a time
        bomb
G HI: Half-Jewish, zany, a painter who turned his
        talents to making money and topographic
        maps; just as I learned to trust him, he turned
        on me
J K: Full-blooded Jew, super-intense, interests:
        music and math, problem: mediocrity

An alphabet soup of lower flames that burned:
    the body flaring up in desire, consuming
    the mind funnelling ashes into urns

Lastly, the man I cannot hate enough, the one I call, in
    polite conversation,

Bad Male Shrink

> ... that
> we can't predict what
> our actions will lead to
> absolves us, tho not
> altogether: . . .
>> A. R. Ammons,
>> *Tape for the Turn of the Year,* 7 Dec:

Let's call him Dr. H or Dr. Hearse, transferred to after my
    first attempt; at first he seemed humane, compassionate
A poor dermatologist is unlikely to do much harm, but a
    bad shrink can be a mortal danger
I remember Dr. H once asking me (he'd prescribed pills
    for my insomnia)
    —You're not going to kill yourself, are you?
    —No, well, not this week!
I remember: Second time in the hospital, calling him from D.C.
    —Help me get out of here, please!
    —How big is the ward, I mean, in square feet?
At their wits' end, the team at Payne Whitney declared
    —Dr. Hearse has absented himself from your case

I've dreamed about torching his office, stealing his book . . .
Catching sight of him on the street
    (he works *and* lives in my neighborhood!)
                  I invent retorts:
    —Still practicing? You still need to
            —I'm fine thanks, no thanks to you
Language, my sword, help me to finish him!
I keep tormenting myself with my part in this:

One day I heard an alarm I dared not heed:
    —You don't care about me as a person, I said on the phone,
        meaning exactly that, *a human being*

His reply: audible irritation, nervous cough
      I knew in his head he'd heard "woman"
Highly verbal, could I have talked him into believing I was
    sane?
I tried to keep faith, desperately needed to . . . grew hostile
   . . . sought to appease him with half-truths . . .
Severely depressed, working my way toward paranoid
    psychosis, I could tune in, read minds (at times these
    readings were confirmed);
        his transmitted: *Get away from me, you bitch!*
No, in retrospect, his knack for not taking me at my word
    when I was *dead serious* was clearly malicious

What have I learned from this?
    My subsequent shrinks have been female
    It is unwise to trust blindly, especially when ill, to entrust
      your living soul to any physician or individual

10 December 1990

> plenty of food & water in
> paradise but some
>   confusion about sex:
> anything so sweet
> should come hard
> as bread & water: . . .
>   A. R. Ammons,
>   *Tape for the Turn of the Year,* 9 Dec:

After a weekend away—D.C.: Titian, Van Dyke, and
friends' new babies—good to be in my own bed again,
aloft, a fearsome height to some men I've been with, a
delight to others, although they must sleep on the edge,
the side with no wall

Out of different times and different mouths:
    —Great to be inside you—some women are too tight,
        others are too loose
    —I had no idea you'd be so athletic
    —I'm afraid I won't satisfy you
    —Get that stuffed animal out of bed!
    —*Tycker du inte om att älska?*
    —Isn't there always some pain involved?
    —You sleep like a statue
                        Stony silence
                                    Soft silence
        Touch alone

Lately, sleeping with bears, remembering someone I wish
        were here, I think, like an animal, about having a mate
But having just been with infants (all weekend I called
        Margaret's Ania "Little Mammal"), happy moms,
        forbearing dads who looked soft and proud but some-
        how excluded

I know it's not a child I want
The man who is not here (yes, another Swede) might do—
    he had the touch
    of someone who loves women

Meanwhile, when unprotected by gay friends, I elude tall
    dark young things who stalk at parties, drinks in hand,
    mouths spilling talk not of making art but the where-
    withal to acquire it: —Too bad I couldn't *buy*
    Strindberg's sketches two years ago . . . Circles are
    small, again we meet, eye each other, do not speak

Horny tonight, I entertain the thought:
    Locked up for a week with an attractive beast
    would I screw him, just like that?

                         Nowadays, probably
not   I want more than *that*

But sometimes the body succumbs, as it does to illness:

Shrinking

I see a woman shrinking, shrinking
    (I don't know what he sees)
physically only   Inside she is bound-
less, open, more knowing than ever
    (I don't know who he sees)

I want you, he says, *wanted you badly*
at first sight—you can't know how much
    (I am a woman rapidly shrinking,
      my body laid out like cloth)
Pinned down under him, I register, mark

his every move, his lines   Out of love,
this first time in months feels odd, an X
movie, an off-Broadway farce
    (Making love to myself
    through a stranger's eyes—
    a narcissistic exercise?)

Younger than he, in years at least, I burn
with luminous calm   The smaller I grow,
the sexier . . . a beacon for lost
boys. What have their fathers done, not done
that they should know nothing of touch?

Can they love us, wanting nothing
but the mothers they have lost? Bodi-
less women, icon and no longer flesh,
eidolon   Skin and bones only, I crack,
recoil, shrinking from his touch

11 December

How to write about men? I've never understood them
Seen through them, yes, loved some, been bored, hurt,
    disappointed, furious, bored
Strange creatures always saying, rarely in so many words:
        Look at me
        Look at what I've done
        Admire and
                Praise
When not Competition or Someone Else to them
 one may be stroked occasionally in return

Not part of my youth in almost any form:
    A house full of women (Mom and Us Three Girls)
    A hardworking father neither absent nor there:
        the latch on the bedroom door meant *Let me work*
                          in peace

I just learned a friend with many sibs is bulimic, says her
    food and sex issues got tangled as she vied for her father's
    attention
        Her father (a doctor who fed her diet pills) is dead
Mine, a man of science, who cared for, treated my mother
    in sickness (unforgettable: her long rambling word-strings,
            weeping, wailing, wandering through the house)
       and (of which, after electroshock, she recalled
            almost nothing)
    in health
        as though she were a bird who loved her cage . . .
Trust him?
        I held him in contempt
                    was not allowed
to show it

Most of my life I've understood nothing but tone

These last few years the family has been taking lessons,
    learning to speak
    in words

18 December

Same old loop: telling the body's
from the mind's possible illness
To what end? Damned if I do; damned
sick last week—lithium level
checked—a virus indeed had caused
headaches and nausea, I turned
on Astrid and her hard disk crashed!
Backed-up but heart-sunk after long
tests, I replaced it. Now, if not
a Hardware Queen, I'm a Princess.
Joyful or distressed, this body
craves systems diagnostics that
will reformat suspect sectors
in memory, find bad clusters,
mark them, display: NO DANGER, at
least report: HEAD SELECT ERROR,
INCORRECTLY INSTALLED HEART

Christmas Day

Started rereading Ammons's long skinny poem last night,
who knows how many more feet of adding-machine tape I
have to go, I'm on page 120 or so. No entries for Christ-
mas eve or day. . . . Some strange ahas, akin to his "saliences."
When he wrote *Tape*, he was my age, also a smoker, and
unemployed. Cornell took him. (They once took me, the
would-be biochemist, but then I got off Yale's waiting list.
I've often wondered if, in Ithaca, I would have remained in
the Sciences, or studied with Ammons, ending up much
the same as I am.)

Stranger still: The way he records what he observes in
nature, the course and discourse of his scientific mind, his
writing on Eros— all resemble Sonnevi's. Now and then, in
different contexts of course, they have written the same
lines.

Even the weather patterns—December lightning, too-
warm days followed by cold—are in accord. And this
morning, in the bare linden tree, a jay.

Questions of Love

> if we were at the
> mercy of what
> we understand,
> our eyes couldn't see:
> A. R. Ammons,
> *Tape for the Turn of the Year*, 31 Dec:

What did I want from them, or they from me,
not just the "men" but the "boys" at school?
Surely not merely physical pleasure—
At age five I discovered masturbation (nameless then)—
  it took some years of late teen-age experience to realize
  men could bestow the pleasure I had alone

Never did learn how to flirt, how to be jealous, dig in my claws,
  hang on (or out)
Only approach I knew (still suffer from) was as an equal
Have lived both sides of seduction, not much fun
All I want is a close friend who's good in bed
  Unheard-of? Too utopian?

So ends the worst year of my life:
Alone still, but hale and sane and fully human
Maybe I could have done more for my departed friends, but
  at no prior time could I have loved them more

My seven-year-old goddaughter (in public school she
  defends how to say my name) informs me now:
    Rika, you know, you're half a kid (Quit pinching my bears!)
    and half a grown-up (Dieting today?)
Do I want to grow *all the way?*

May the new year bring new leaves, better times
Resolved, in the interim:
    To be adult: severing attachments that no longer serve
    To be childlike: trusting those I love will never leave

Subtexts

1. The Beginning

She tells a friend:
—I've met someone who seems interested in me,
an economist, not a bad writer,
a bit old perhaps, and Jewish,
with terrible posture, but there's something . . .
I like the sound of his voice.

—In you as a woman or as a writer?

Baffled (naive perhaps), she answers:
—Don't know.

2. From Down Under

He sends his poems. (She sends some of hers.)
They talk on the phone, go out a couple of times.
Patches of common ground emerge, in which strange little
    flags get planted from the first:

- Displays his treasures—Yeats autographs, an old
  edition of Donne, a millennial bronze vessel the size
  of her palm—all at once, as if she'd never return.
- Will not hear of sickness, has had enough of it in his
  life.
- Reports his income. Says for six years he was analyzed
  by a famous shrink, learned nothing. Implies that his

underlying never-clinical depression (which he now
treats with drugs) is responsible for his not quite
making it in life.

• Has spent two decades here, still can't hear the chime
of *mother* with *desire*.

3. A Mighty Fortress

Still, she barely knows him, wants to give Chance a chance,
knows too well how swiftly she can become *eine feste Burg*;
asks him over for Sunday afternoon. He accepts.
Hours to be arranged, he'll call.

More texts come, in a postscript he writes:
—Why not assume (when reading my poems) that I know
what I'm doing most of the time, and comment on when
I'm succeeding or failing in my intentions?

She replies by card (*Reconciliation Elegy*, Motherwell):
—Your mind's mirror I cannot be, and then,
there's the fallacy of intention . . .

below her signature,
Supercollider, Inc.

Thinks of her friends who take her as she is; in a novel
    by one of them, her namesake is a 7-year-old "beautiful
    monster."
Thinks of Captain Picard on the *Enterprise*, thrusting his forearm
    forward as he gives the command: *Engage!*

4. Withholding

Sunday at 10 the phone:
—When shall I come over?
—Not having heard from you, I made other plans.
—How can that be? I wrote it here, in my diary . . .

Rather solitude than the straitjacket
of being asked blindly to give
                              (friendship, help, or love?)
something to someone bound
to refuse or deny.

5. The Rewrite

Monday all day she writes a text like this one. Feels bad
—though the choice was right—having done what she'd done.
Returns from dinner to his message: *Please call.*

It takes time. She explains the concept of "use," the term
    "friend" (not applicable to them).
He reads her passages of her poems he has rewritten
    as if they were his own.
One thing is clear: Whatever he wants of her is (at best) unclear:
—Perhaps we should lay poetry aside . . .
May I call you again, say, in a week's time?

6. The Game

Time passes. Life goes on. She dislikes unfinished
business, sends an essay she promised him on Celan. Wants
the tidiness, the closure of 0 for 3.

They'll meet for a film and dinner; a few hours before,
he cancels the meal; he's been asked to a seder,
    does not invite her.

The Doors starts late (her focus: Morrison's
leather-clad hips), lasts long.
Even his accent has begun to grate on her.
And it's more than uncomfortable
avoiding all talk of what has long been,
more than a profession, the saving center
    of her life.

7. Easter Sunday: The End?

Not the sole center but the one that holds.

This year the holy days coincide:
    Passover without Simone to sing *Dayyenu.*
    Holy Saturday without Matt and eggs to dye.

Easter Sunday, again the Passion spins.
Could she believe, it would be in Resurrection.

8. Two Weeks Later

Einsamkeit/ensamhet: Each day an anniversary
    she would forget, not celebrate.
Loneliness, though she's always disapproved of any
    word for the above but "solitude."
Where is she now? And where are all her friends?
    Her goddaughter is off in—where was it? Disneyland?

Work remains:
        Sonnevi—
the "unending" poem—all his books reread,
she spins down his gyres, deeper in, ever
suspicious of the bird's-eye view,
               verges on
writing, scrubs the bath; as the water whirls
down the drain, the phone:

[Him again:] —I'll be downtown, in search of your Rilke; lunch?

9. Absence makes . . . no bedfellows

Wanting company, caring little about the rest, she relaxes,
    observes.
Reticent about her person, he stalks her bookshelves, duly
    impressed; plays with her wind-ups.
In this she reads an attraction (to a woman and a writer?),
    and a studied avoidance of betraying the signs.

Might she be mistaken?

On parting, he touches her hands.

No History

1. Control

He hands her a line that makes her laugh; she
grasps it all right, from her usual distance
extends a hand, for once with an open heart.
They talk, they laugh; things start
to come to a head.
                    Aroused but unready, un-
willing to discount her own heart's tempo, she
slows things down.

Next day a lion bounds out of its lair; his last affair—
        "Binding and dark, there was blood," he says, "no chains"
                (none visible to the eye)—
        (to her ears) more an addiction than a relation.
Is it her gift to prompt men to display their worst early on?
        And, if so, why?

Her mind weighs the knowledge; in the balance, losses she
        could cut.
                Oh, to shut down the mind, its warnings. It's easy
                to heed warnings. (She's nothing if not smart.)

When he declares the decision to be hers and she asks what
        he means and no answer comes, she doubts they'll
        survive another day.
                They?

Strike one?
    Preemptive?
        All's fair . . .
                that ends . . .
                        Well,

is this mere wordplay, verbal push and pull
or some wild experiment without a control?

See you at the theater tomorrow, she hears herself say,
    thinks: let this play be just a play.

2. Arena

He regrets his disclosure, says:
—Listen, today's a new day.

    (If a tree falls in the forest . . . Can words
    once said and heard be silent, cease to report
    to impinge on all those uttered before or since?
    What question is simple or ever was?)

He remains charming but vulgar, a nonstop tease.
She tries to be natural, "herself," is not at ease.

The object (seen through her eyes' dark rounds):
    To maneuver her into the ring, a labyrinth,
    To bridle his beast with kindness, warmth.

3. Words

Draw, standoff, deadlock, tied
for no place. She dreams his image—
nothing precise, wakes with but one
word droning in her mind: TROUBLE.

Might they be "friends"? Barring
the sexual pull, it all seems so
unlikely. A friend of hers who knows
him slightly opines "inappropriate."

Another says: —Sweetie, are you so very hungry?
You've come too far, dropped too much weight to sink
your teeth into some hunk stuffed with problems;
spit him out; there will be other morsels.

Could the witch resist Hansel,
knowing she'd burn out?
*Oh, how sweet it was to feel
desirous and desirable.*

Why had he spilled his beans
before she cared
to know? People say—do—
strange things.

Binding and dark—let's see,
a cummerbund?
A tight black bra and girdle?
Words chosen,

to startle, entertain, disgust?
Writers! They would
just as soon live in imagination
as anywhere

made up of flesh and blood.

Interviews

Subject

In the story you tell about me I am not
to be trusted   I hurt you years before we met
remain a familiar you can't recognize
Fast-forwarded reenactment viewed through gauze

In the story I tell about you there is
disappointment I also took you for some-
body else (someone with more regard for life)
The interview a crossroads:
                        In my home you
asked questions   I responded   And we came close
to making love   (I have learned, if not patience,
caution   To slow the action of desire, a
nonspecific drug)

                    This is not the whole story
We met here last fall, in your country in summer
You were not well   I was your guest   I watched you eat
and drink yourself toward death

Predicate

Chance, my old friend, brings us together again
back on this side—Columbia, then Yale   Talk
between us seems possible   But you soon take

refuge in the crushing weight of silence or
the irresponsible slur of alcohol

Between us now—not friendship—strategies:
Out of ambivalence hate or love (I can
only postulate a motive) you send an
emissary equipped with tape recorder
agenda of his own, intellectual
and otherwise   Young bright   Blue bedroom eyes I
am not really interested though the game
intrigues me   Another checkpoint not -mate   You
both fly home

And I write to you as if nothing happened
(was nothing to me something more to him?)
as if you cared how things went
(why do I think you would?)
because stories like these—inconclusive
hushed, tortuous—require an end

CAN ZONE
or
THE GOOD FOOD GUIDE

What do you mean, you "don't like poetry"?
Did someone force you, as a child, to taste
rancid stanzas, tainted, reeking lines, so poetry
made you sick (not at heart but) to your stomach? Poetry
laid on thick, like peanut butter, may take
its time dissolving on your palate. Poetry
thin as gruel's unpalatable. Still, poetry
made well, like a fine soufflé, will rise and stand.
How can I make a herbivore understand
that words are flesh *and* grass in poetry,
fish and fowl, birdflight, signs we read,
transforming themselves and us because we read?

Twelve years ago in the *Tribune* I happened to read
about GIANT BOLIVIAN FROGS. Of them I made poetry.
Frenchmen canned them, leaving enough to breed,
while chefs the world over steamed, roasted, grilled, and
     decreed:
No other known creature has such an unusual taste
or transmutable texture. And then the rumors spread:
*BIG FROGS RADIOACTIVE! THE DEVIL'S OWN EGGS! DRED-
GE LAKE TITICACA!* The strangest tales take
shape in poetry. Put down your *Times* and take
less heed of current events. In Ovid you'll read
how the will to change could help a girl withstand
indecent advances. See, by the pond, that stand

of laurels— "Croak!" blurts a frog. "Old myths don't stand
a chance in the—blouagh—modern world! Let's read
of true metamorphoses. Once we had to stand
in for a human prince; but our royal stand-
ard bore a crowned frog salient, King of Poetry!
Marianne Moore, who showed a firm understand-
ing of the natural order, took the witness stand
in behalf of our cousins (she had discerning taste):
In 'imaginary gardens' (not really to our taste)
place 'real toads'; they, warts and all, set stand-
ards for poetry. Subjects, be literal, take
us at our word. Nothing can be worth tak-

ing that serves but once. Amphibians always take
new leases on life; we are its double stand-
ard. Snakes shed their skins, but only we will take
ours off and eat them. Survive! Make no mistake,
on land, in water, you've got to learn to read
between the lines. Don't eat my words, take
them to heart: Leaps, turns, liberties, take
them all; change and be changed or poetry
will die!" Double-talk? Free speech? What else but poetry
encompasses so much? What else can take
bitter experience and camouflage its taste
so we may feed and live and breathe and taste

the next sunrise? What other art can make us taste
what we see: the golden egg whose rising we take
for granted, or set our sights on goose (tast-
ier still) all at once, prodding our taste

buds (smell those cracklings!), forcing our senses to stand
up and take notice? What else awakens taste
for the fruits of knowledge or plants an aftertaste
of first things in apples bitten and apples read?
What but this art can keep our daily bread
from going stale in our mouths?
                                        "To each his taste,"
you say; I'm hungry and all this talk of poetry
won't fill my gut!" —That only proves poetry

's power of suggestion. "But what if poetry
still gives me indigestion?" —A little taste
will surely settle the question. "What do you take
me for, a guinea pig?" —A hungry child who can't stand
being fed. The world's your oyster. Open wide, now. Read.

Commentary and Notes

This collection takes its title from a poem written in 1975, close to half my life ago. I wrote most of these poems in the 1970s, and for some time they formed the manuscript of what was to be my "first book." But then the poems of *Etruscan Things* (1983) broke through and declared themselves a through-composed and more satisfactory whole to my sensibility at the time. Given the choice of which to publish by mentor and angel Richard Howard, I chose the speaking objects of art to speak for me in *my* first book of poems. I had already published translations of Rilke and Ekelöf; I was much influenced by how each of Ekelöf's books—I translated only his last—was so different from the preceding one.

In the 1980s, I broke down but came back to life writing another unitary volume, *All We Need of Hell* (1995). In the early '90s, one or more versions of that manuscript contained poems from the "About Men" section, beginning with "PAGES TOWARD THE TURN OF THE YEAR." The only poems from the '80s are "Away" and the final canzone, a rhapsody on poetry and food.

Given the opportunity to gather these "uncollected" poems into a book—"letting go of these will release you to write a new one," Richard insists—it has helped to bear in mind that Göran Sonnevi, the Swedish poet I have been translating in sickness and in health since late 1983, considers all his work—now thirteen books of poems—to be part of one single long poem.

p. 4—"The Amy Lowell Voluntary Exile." In 1974–75 I lived in Sweden as the recipient of the John Courtney Murray Fellowship from Yale and the Amy Lowell Poetry Traveling Scholarship. The latter stipulated that I write at least three poems and remain outside North America for twelve months; I did not opt to renew for a second year.

Fortschritt (German): progress.

Utlandagatan: Out-country Street (in both senses of the word).

språkvård: the preservation of the purity of the language.

p. 7—"Prescriptions from Sleeplessness." Gunnar Ekelöf (1907–1968) is widely considered the greatest Swedish lyric poet of the twentieth century. Four poems in his *Guide to the Underworld* begin with the phrase *"Ensam i tysta natten"* ["Alone in the quiet night"]. (See also notes to "Losses" and "Khalaf-al-Akhmar, the Truth-Liar.")

regn och blåst: rain and wind.

vintersolståndet: the winter solstice.

julskinka: Swedish baked Christmas ham.

"a carton of Kex": Gina's and my idiolect for a packet of bland, round, plain cookies.

p. 11—"Losses." Ekelöf also wrote several collections of essays. This poem interprets "A Photograph," a memoir of his father published first in *Verklighetsflykt* (Flight from Reality, 1958), now in volume six of his eight-volume *Works*.

Panayía, Átokos, and *Fatumeh* are predominantly divine female figures who appear chiefly in his Diwan trilogy, whose first two books were translated by W. H. Auden and Leif Sjöberg and appear almost in their entirety in *Gunnar Ekelöf: Selected Poems,* Penguin Modern European Poets series, 1971. The last, *Guide to the Underworld* (1967), is available from the University of Massachusetts Press in my translation (1980).

p. 14—"Værøy." My visit to Lofoten took place in the summer of 1975. More than twenty years later, trying to check on the spelling of *Kalkluovnen* I recorded in my journal, I have learned the rock formation has several variant spellings, pronunciations, and possible etymologies. This has made me considerably more sympathetic to Poe.

p. 24—"Departures." The subtitles of the poem's three sections taken together form the first line of Rilke's "Requiem for a Friend" (in memory of Paula Modersohn-Becker): "I have Dead, and I let them go." The quotation in section three is from the same poem.

"Departures" was also included in *All We Need of Hell* (University of North Texas Press, 1995).

Recently I have learned that in Middle and Modern Persian my first name means "desired, beloved, lover," and "a class of ushers at a royal court"; in a northern Persian dialect it also means "boy."

p. 32—"Under the Roof." Where Henry Street meets Clark Street, the Hotel Saint George continues to battle the trains of the 7th Avenue IRT.

p. 39—"Khalaf-al-Akhmar, the Truth-Liar." Khalaf-al-Akhmar (or Chalef elahmar ben hajjan) lived in the eighth century, in Basra and Kufa, among other places. Ekelöf identifies him as "one of the great Arabian bards." See "A shadow said: / My name was Khalaf-al-Akhmar" in *Guide to the Underworld*.

p. 56—"PAGES TOWARD THE TURN OF THE YEAR." The unit of composition for this poem was the journal page, the capacious A4 journal page, allowing for long, unbroken, and nonwrapping lines, far more easily mimicked on $8^{1}/_{2}$-x-11-inch paper than in the diminutive pages of this book itself. I want to thank the Press for working with me where linear rearrangement was necessary.

The poem opens with *"Men are //* largely absent from

this book" because it was conceived as part of *All We Need of Hell*. Astrid, my computer in the "18 December" section, is an old AST Premium 286.

p. 69—"Subtexts." This poem was also written contemporaneously with those in *All We Need of Hell*; more about the dying friends in section seven can be found there, especially in "Life: It Must Suffice Us."
Göran Sonnevi, Swedish poet b. 1939. In the eighth section I describe working on the introduction to *A Child Is Not a Knife: Selected Poems of Göran Sonnevi* (Princeton, 1993).

The James Dickey Contemporary Poetry Series
Edited by Richard Howard

Error and Angels
Maureen Bloomfield

Portrait in a Spoon
James Cummins

The Land of Milk and Honey
Sarah Getty

All Clear
Robert Hahn

Growing Back
Rika Lesser

Traveling in Notions: The Stories of Gordon Penn
Michael J. Rosen

United Artists
S. X. Rosenstock

The Threshold of the New
Henry Sloss